MOTH HOUR

MOTH HOUR
ANNE KENNEDY

AUCKLAND
UNIVERSITY
PRESS

First published 2019
Auckland University Press
University of Auckland
Private Bag 92019
Auckland 1142
New Zealand
www.press.auckland.ac.nz

© Anne Kennedy, 2019

ISBN 9 781 86940 894 7

Published with the assistance of
Creative New Zealand

A catalogue record for this book is available from
the National Library of New Zealand

This book is copyright. Apart from fair dealing for
the purpose of private study, research, criticism or
review, as permitted under the Copyright Act, no
part may be reproduced by any process without
prior permission of the publisher. The moral rights
of the author have been asserted.

Design by Kalee Jackson

Cover photography by Caryline Boreham

Photograph on p. 103: Philip Kennedy c.1971
at the family house at Island Bay, Wellington.
Photograph by Matthew Kennedy

Printed in Singapore by Markono Print Media
Pte Ltd

This book is dedicated, with love, to my siblings Margaret Mary (Wellington), Matthew (1942–1996), James (New Jersey, USA), Peter (Räterschen, Switzerland), Philip (1951–1973) and Richard (Frome, UK).

One who has trodden this garden path cannot fail to remember how his spirit, as he walked in the twilight of evergreens over the regular irregularities of the stepping stones, beneath which lay dried pine needles, and passed beside the moss-covered granite lanterns, became uplifted above ordinary thoughts.
 – Kakuzo Okakura, *The Book of Tea*

Death, slowly moving among the bleached clouds,
knows us better than we know ourselves.
 – Adrienne Rich, 'Moth Hour'

CONTENTS

Foreword   9

Thirty-Three Transformations on a Theme of Philip   11

The *Thé*   71

Pattern/Chaos: An Afterword   85

Notes   99

Acknowledgements   101

FOREWORD

On Guy Fawkes night, 1973, my brother Philip was partying on a hillside section in Wellington when he accidentally fell to his death. He was twenty-two. He had been a reader, a talker, an epileptic, a history-buff, an alcoholic, a political apologist with a short fuse, and a poet.

The family didn't know what to do about grief. The noisy house went silent. I was fourteen. I lay on the red rug in the sitting room and listened to Beethoven's *Thirty-Three Variations on a Waltz by Anton Diabelli*, op. 120 – over and over, because it was there. (Our uncle had died the year before, and his classical record collection had been added to the house soundtrack of rock and pop.) Over six months, I listened to how the waltz transformed into things that were funny, sad, outrageous, and in the end, epic. Beethoven had gone on a tour of his musical influences – Ludwig van Beethoven, This is Your Life.

There were seven siblings. Philip was in the middle. I was the youngest. Peter is the closest in age to Philip and the one who nicknamed him 'Moth' as a child – perhaps because he was quick and annoying and cast a shadow. A few weeks after the death, Peter brought Philip's things to the family house at Island Bay. In the big, light bunk room they had shared as children, he shuffled books onto the white school-woodwork bookcase as if returning them to their tūrangawaewae.

Over the next couple of years, I read these books. They'd been culled. I knew that because I remembered what had been there before Philip moved out of home, and because there was nothing he liked better than a rave about books. There was no Bertrand Russell, no Beat poets, no American School, no Zukofsky, Gertrude Stein, T. S. Eliot or Sylvia Plath. There was no Dylan Thomas, whom Philip loved so much as a teen that he tried to be Dylan Thomas by drinking a lot – then suddenly, like a misguided affair, went off him. No Yeats (his 'moth-hour of eve'), no Shelley, no Walter Benjamin. There was: James K. Baxter, Günter Grass, Brendan Behan, Timothy Leary, Herman Hesse, a French dictionary, a Kafka novella about a creature you might put in a jar, *The Book of Changes*, and a much-pencilled edition of *The Book of Tea*.

Also on Philip's bookcase: a manila envelope containing a manuscript of poems typed in Courier on thick, cream, letter-sized paper.

The following variations riff (like Beethoven) off one of Philip's poems.

THIRTY-THREE TRANSFORMATIONS ON A THEME OF PHILIP

THE *THE*ME

Come catch me little child
and put me in a jar.

Place inside:
        some leaves (for me to eat)
        The Book of Tea (for me to read)
        some paper,
            any paper
        and a pen (for me to write)

Screw on the top,
      little child,
and put six airholes in the lid,
then leave me on your windowsill.

Just one more thing,
      little child,
look through your sunset hair
into my world
before I die
and collect your imaginary mind.

        Philip Kennedy *c.* 1970

THE TRANSFORMATIONS

1.

The thing in the jar
always dies!

The rice cooker steams
so the sun goes down

Deep in the house
sepia gathers

The pencil has eaten
the fragile book

2.

(for me to eat)
        in the first place
        a gulp of air
            please give me
            the meaningful paper

(for me to read)
        the spider's web
            at its centre
            a black dot
        the moon is setting

(for me to write)
        a strange dream
            transformed
            in fuzzy pencil
        the lampshade ticks
        with moth bodies

(for me to walk)
        the seam on a shirt
        the purple arteries
            of the city streets

(for me to want)
        to know you always
            invisible thing
        throw three coins
        to find the changes

3.

catch me / if can
think think / if can't

if can / a jar
if not / an air

take my hand / if can
if can't / second thoughts

in a garden / if there
if not / a room

think think / if can
if can't / dream

any dream / any jar
any number / reasons

hold me / any me
in the first place / if can

the second place / is
the whole / fucking point

in a jar / if can
if can't / imagine

4.

The new sun rushes
              the dead trees
Your white breath moves
in and out of the lung duplex

I put my thoughts
              on the Kingsland train
A family with boxes tumbles
in and out of the shaky real estate

At the edge of the lawn
              a plastic letterbox
like a Venus flytrap
eats a letter from the courts

Apples plummet
            from a split bag
the floor awash
with bruises and freedom

A child's face
              remembers the bedrooms
the released cat
fights its new neighbourhood

The garden path
            leads to the garden
all roads
to the brother's sunset

5.

Some footsteps any footsteps
some garden any garden
jar any jar
this jar

Some paper any paper
a pen any pen
room any room
this room

Read some feed any feed
drink wine any red
laugh any laugh
           this rage

And if some body any body
arch any back
lift any belly
           but this sweat

At some party any party
this crowd any dance
witch any Sabbath
           but this death

6.

Tamarillos ornaments on the kitchen sill

all day red and all day warm

as touch
                as factory

by the cool glass, the white paintwork

all the trouble begins.

7.

Coming down off the spine of the botanical gardens
onto the green flank of the dragon, shadows arch

under my feet. In the dell below, the shell-shaped stage
is strewn with red camellias. November

and across the valley on the dense dark Tinakori Hill
houses begin to light up like Guy Fawkes.

At the top of Patanga Crescent the pared-down villa
trembles with young men thinking,

pens lost in the wide sleeves of their dead uncles.
They are ecstatic and do everything extravagantly

in the last light: read, drink, fuck.
On the windowsill – a stone, leaf, a twig with buds,

and the black cat left behind mewling by the old lady
now in the Home of Compassion. No change.

8.

They drink the contents of houses in the subdivisions
a glittering view of the harbour while the Gatsby-dads

are up at the beach. The boys from Saint Pats town,
where they raised them up and tore them down

like statues – the grey angles of their uniforms – who saw
the spectre of the little nun collecting for the poor,

find they have a great love for the transubstantiating
power of plenty. Their placards rest in the passage:

Stay Away LBJ. Sometimes they come down long enough
to need drugs to sleep at night. Every so often

I meet a boomer who was at the party on the hill
that night – a girl dancing barefoot in purple velvet

and flowers, off her face on the lawn –
and she will tell me her version of the fall.

9.

Letter to Philip in Heaven or Hell or on the cloud
of unknowing. We're still suspended here, as ever.

The kids — descendants of Irish peasants, like you are,
Philip — on a sunny afternoon unearth black clods

from their laptops and are in love with the sudden light.
They are in despair at the rottenness of the earth

and of governments. WTF. They're also, of course,
of this earth, the great-great-grandchildren

of tohunga from Tai Tokerau, of Kai Tahu fisher folk.
The boy sees his father some Mondays for a hamburger.

The girl walks the dog around Grey Lynn at sunset.
Pray for them. But generally they are okay. Eileen

goes back to Otago, and Tem's friend Patu swings by
in the evening and they share some beers and a game.

10.

In a jar on the sill

leaf and pen

a wild party

11.

You don't need to be an alcoholic to be a poet.
That has been well established as a thing.
With your mind straight, go, go into the next moment.

Though poets before you may have drained the Moët
and penned lines in a heightened state of ping,
you don't actually need to be an alcoholic to be a poet

or a drug addict to be a gardener. Just do it,
unearth earth in your fingers and see what that will bring.
With your mind straight, go, go into the next moment.

Don't worry that in your attempts to love you will blow it.
There is no love but the next ring.
You don't need to be an alcoholic to be a poet

or a man, for that matter, or a white know-it-
all. Anyone can put on the tea kettle and sing.
Go, go straightly into the next moment.

My brother, if you're out there, if you foment
your eternity in a fissure of song, speed, an angel's wing
you'll know you don't need to be an alcoholic to be a poet,
that with your mind straight you go into the next moment.

12.

One more thing
the sun is going down
the waistcoats seemed like progress
the love song was divine
but the sun is going down.

The afternoons seem longer
are pleasantly laid out
a cool mall
all that you can tweet
but the sun is descending rapidly.

Sea levels lap like baptism
we run screaming from the building
the campus managers are thieves
their fingerprints are on the poetry
the lip of the horizon has gone green.

Will you make a nest of pens?
Will you grow your shady fringe
or drink a cup of equanimity?

Talk talk
the loved ones in your phone
as the night roars on
watch the moonlight pick its favs
put it back no it's too late.
Safe in its prison
that thing you took.

13.

The marriage was a farm. In spring
babies appeared like blue trembling lambs
wrangled from sex and blood and slime.

They fattened ruthlessly, little temples for the soul.
Except for the sixth, born on a brutal winter's day.
He stared death absurdly down the barrel.

The mother saved his life four times, not counting frenzies.
Wai worry? His eternity, his name down
for the Catholic school. And no, it was only twice.

Summertime, three years to heaven, the little death wish
triked a mile to the sea. Do unto me.
They plucked him off the rocks like a pipi.

Aged four, and croup as thick as a cork,
she wrapped him like a Lenten statue and called a taxi.
They rode where the wind blows wild.

Then and there in the waiting room,
as a waiter or a plumber does, they opened him.
The demigods rushed in.

Oh the parties! Body and soul, light and dark,
a Maui or an Erlking's trick. Drunk. The blue of sky
seen through the airhole in his lid.

One time he swallowed a bottle of pearls.
Death the rage, he the rager. He didn't really mean it.
He'd left a trail in the forest, but birds ate them.

We were the fantails, my brother and me, thirteen and ten,
flitting. We found him raving and quickly fading.
Before the funeral flowers, we called our mother.

In the bedroom doorway, she wrung her hands.
So many and so many. The lambs. The trouble I see.
'I've saved his life twice already. Shall we leave him?'

She didn't really mean it. Drunk. Our howls,
efficient as a god's, still shook the hills at dawn.
One last time, intensive care, questions, questions.

Turn him off, or keep him on, like Karen Ann?
Like a sheep, bred for death, they let him go
into the bardo.

14.

I wish I was a bug
I wish I had a jar

One two three four five six
Oh play the blue guitar

I wish I knew for sure
Will thinking do the trick?

In this world and the next
You are you are you are

I wish I had a room
I wish I had a book

Throw it back again
I don't know where to look

What could we have done?
And what can we do now?

One two three four five six
One two three four five six

I wish I want I take
I wish I had a jar.

15.

Fall floors me
I'm all ooh aah
I'd forgotten how
one day in April
a little gold death

kills the leaves

the air takes off
like a jet
and lands again

the trees creak
their aching news
among the wires

and a book left
on a bench
is skim-read
by a cloud

I'd forgotten
how fall
remembers other falls
like blurred photographs
and early sunsets
through your hair

that sadness
is exciting
little April little death
I'd forgotten
fall
its wild future
waiting there.

16.

Way down in the Antipodes
where English settlers raised their meat
a boy called Philip Kennedy
read history lest we repeat.

One moth hour he wormed from a book
a factoid of last century –
a Churchill buck fresh off the boat
had rustled sheep in Canterbury.
              (New Zealand, that is.)

Caught red-handed with the wool –
blood of the lamb, blood on his hands –
the thief was strung up as a fool.
Sad end for the remittance man.

But Philip felt his heartbeat skip
– he'd been reading recently
how Winston Churchill's tribe had shipped
a wild son to the colony.

Thinking Winnie'd like to log
the fate of long lost Uncle Church
Philip wrote the old Bulldog
the fruits of his research.

Reply was quick to Master Phil
Kennedy, The South Seas. 'Be
assured no inverse Churchill
bore any relationship to me'
              (a British Churchill, that is)

signed The Former Naval Person.
Whateva, it just got better –
Phil in the paper, white and nerdy,
holding up his Churchill letter.

At the wake (dusk fell) they tell
the Philip tales – his wild streak,
his braininess, and hell,
how the colonial boy wrote back.

Fun fact: Winston Churchill was sworn in as Premier
of the United Kingdom for the first time on 10 May 1940.
Philip was born on the same day eleven years later.

17.

The marvellous child
lives in the slow year

the bright lawn
seethes with rugby

the dinner plates
half meat

brains
have their own wild
chemistry

mostly
the yellow days are flat
the flickering night-times
roll downhill

a page
crushes a minute

look at the stars
(little child)

dead roses
and a quote:
(turn on, tune in, drop out)

but don't
really mean it

the sweet workingsout
as on a guitar

you are you are you are

18.

Thin blue hoodie boy
leaving the party

jingle in your pocket:
                              bottlecaps (the casings)
                              key (for a dark house)
                              some paper
                                          any papers
                              tremble (and cry)

Lonely in the moonlight
                              blue boy
punch your own lights out
paint the bottle shop blue.

One more thing,
        (*Da ba de!*)
rage through your pūkana
if you can
if you can stand
and take back your impounded dream.

19.

Catch me little child and put me in a jar.

Ajar is small and a view of everything.

Hopefully we will always want and want for nothing.

Shall I seize you? Yes, I mean no. Please seizure.

We will live in a jar.

I will live in a jar. And the jar is a house.

Place inside a place inside.

That is how we will look out. Look out.

I am being very straight with you.

Look no hands.

In the language.

Who's talking then? Who am I talking to?

Please please seize me.

It is all mine. That's what I anyway want today.

My eyes rolling. The floor is my friend.

Another day, another suitcase.

Some leaves for me to eat.

I will leave never to return anything.

I don't know if I am thing or child thing or child.

You are child.

Or seizure. In the grip of the imagination.

Run away with the images.

Do be quiet. No don't be. Be.

I will read the veins almost.

The calligraphy.

Paper any paper any paper will be the sum total

my disbelief and my leaves.

When that happens, I will give you a pen to eat.

Thank write you. I will never forget

the trouble I've seen you've seen.

It, the seizing, is all worth it. It.

I never throw a piece of paper upon which I have written,

is what was really said and always.

Because never in my life had there been

or will be

or always will be.

Screw on the top, little child.

My head is my friend and my friendship.

Where have you gone really?

Happy birthday, May, by the way,

in a school uniform and the flailing limbs, the thump

and day in November.

I remember the sea, the sea wall,

the grains, the shattering.

I don't want it to be the talked-about thing,

seizing to be the seizure,

imaging to be the imagination sum of it. It.

One is one and one is the other and two.

Put six airholes in the lid.

One two three four five six

then leave me on your windowsill.

I can see everything open will open up will foam at the mouth.

We will remember the Famine but I hope not.

I hope you will not. Tenderly

how I mean it, because hopefulness.

Hopeless and hopeful is about.

I will sleep all day. The night half of it cut and dark with sleep.

Just one more thing, which is

all the windowsills,

little child.

Look through your sunset hair

into my world before I die,

I hope not too soon hoping like hell,

you said and I accidently said

hoping for no tripping and tumbling accidents.

Full of tenderness for you and it and always

because so young!

Aue aue aue!

Away away away.

I am going away with the.

If there is a day, a seizure and the night will be there.

Sometimes my mind sets like the sun

was what he wrote,

and never throw away a leaf

or jar, but it is burst and eternally bursting

and you and I and one.

Seize me

and collect your imaginary mind.

When I wake you will wake,

it will be the wake.

20.

                I don't think I can come
to your party
                The surface of the tea
                is oily with sky

The urgent sentences
die on the slow paper
                I have no pleasure in reporting any of this

At the polytech the deceitful executives feed books
like Trump-coal to the runaway train
                In Santa hats they chortle at the teachers
                their fat salaries spilled down their shirtfronts

Loving a liar is like having bulimia
The psychedelic fountain is wise
                The wind and the rain are recycled
The woman of the dunes loves her sand

At the bookcase the spines are a garden
I choose a green fuse
                What pluck!

You tumble backwards like a diver
The waters close like a zip
                The underworld is soundless with ideas
                thoughts return to the wild

How can you burst back into sunlight?

I don't know I don't know

I hope to attend one of your parties
before I die
your death has already
been established

21.

1.

On the streets of Wellington Mother Aubert is collecting for the poor
with her pram which has no baby, and that's quite creepy although
her intentions are good. The poor are the ones not collecting, you can
spot them a mile off because they don't have a pram. If they do
the pram will have a baby — well not have a baby, but have a baby in it.
They are all normal, everything about them is normal. But their
sleeves are probably empty, it's hard to tell, but they are most likely
empty of everything except arms. I find that unaccountably sad.
Boo hoo! Even though I'm much the same myself. What we could all
do is read a book of poetry every day. With a badge on your chest
stating your business. Begin today! I'm going to, I'm going to begin
with Anna Jackson. It will do you good, it will do everybody good.

2.

Someone is playing a guitarful of Dylan songs on the record player
in the living room. He's brilliant, Bob, although he does whine.
If he didn't whine we might not notice his brilliance. It's one of those
conundrums like a tree falling in the forest with no one to see it.
Or the colour of a chair. We'll never know whether it's red or blue.
You'd see the tree the next day if you went on a walk specifically
to propose marriage to someone. You'd both (hopefully there
are two of you) see the tree. Or did you just dream it?

3.

People mean well but they just keep getting drunk all the time and
making a hash of things. Six airholes in a lid will probably not
be nearly enough, yet there is plenty of air, there is no prohibition
of air as far as I know. And the insect, the insect will die. I tell you
we must die. The needle exchange is a good idea. Gardens are
a cliché but that's because they're so good. It takes a long time
for the sun to go down.

4.

If someone told you to collect your imaginary mind as opposed
to the one made of blood and guts, you'd do it, right? Although
sometimes it's hard to tell them apart. But you must at least try.
That is actually all there is to it, says Philip.

22.

Oh Beethoven, your hero Napoleon's one for the road

was one too many. I need the loo just thinking about it.

In an earthquake the plaster cherubs at the town hall

sieve down, but we will drink the unexploded beer.

Can you make a jolly omelette without piercing

the scared heart? Horror films are best viewed through

Venetian blinds, a shelf of toys, a jar – sexual abuse

through a pudding-bowl fringe. The exorbitant coffin

will be paid for by the grandchildren of immigrants.

For sale online, a set of turned piano legs, little used.

23.

Come catch me little child
and put me in a jar
and I will be your guide
though I will be your prisoner
and from the place of wanting
and clawing I'll be your discovery
and I will discover trees in bloom
when they are in bloom
in sepia when they are not
and bees humming and dying
in a room and then I will or you will
write about them and lament
and I will knit and you will wear
a pussy hat to show that we
lament and act and together
guide and prisoner
we will imagine.

24.

Hire a car from VroomVroomVroom
and drive into the afternoon
make a nest of love and knees
and shove in all your fav CDs

Green blur
you make my heart stir,
car bling
you make me sing.

Bring some tea and raspberry tarts,
all the songs you know by heart.
Pack a notebook and a pen
in case you end up feeling Zen.

Green blur
you make my heart stir,
car bling
you make me sing.

(Bring a pen,
feeling Zen.)

Tap into the GPS
the rhythm to a green address.
For a wandering mind, just see
directions from *The Book of Tea*.

All around you is the grey
of the urban motorway,
but you have a sense of cool
as you burn your fossil fuel.

Oh green blur
you make my heart stir,
car bling
you make me sing.

(GPS,
green address,
sense of cool,
fossil fuel.)

Finally, it's country roads.
He sings 'Like a Rolling Stone',
hurtling forwards, going wow,
remembering the birth canal.

Did you ever fall in love?
Did you ever cut a nerve?
Playing dead not feel a thing?
Really, real – you make me sing!

Green blur
you make my heart stir,
car bling
you make me sing.

(Going wow,
birth canal,
feel a thing,
make me sing.)

Hooks and bait are in the trunk –
never know, the fish might jump.
There's a blanket so the grass
doesn't poke you up the arse.

Hit the spot and settle in.
Pretend you've set up house with him.
Stuff your face and stuff your cunt,
but do beware, it's just a stunt.

Green blur
you make my heart stir,
car bling
you make me sing.

(So the grass,
up your arse,
stuff your cunt,
just a stunt.)

Then it's dark and then you purl
down the Rimutaka hill.
No more floating, no more mirth,
like Uncle Albert, down-to-earth.

Sure you had a lovely day,
screwed the planet on the way.
Do you think I fucking care?
I'm one tired teddy bear.

*Green blur
you make my heart stir,
car bling
you make me sing,
oh green blur
you make my heart stir,
car bling
you make me sing.*

(No more mirth,
down-to-earth,
fucking care,
teddy bear.)

Green blur

you make my heart stir,

car bling

you make me sing.

25.

Crushed the grass and broke the web

Blurred the air and faked the stream

Hate and greed, decision deed

I was there, I hate that

In the garden sexist shit

It's so cold, I need my coat

Trample twigs, have your say

By postal vote, by Post-it note

Gather the landscape in a jar

All is see-through, all is love

See my fist, here it comes

This is the end of the rhetorical situation

26.

Accident you came upon
                that night the phone call

The matte phone, the dark hall
                  your white nightie, the frantic friend

But my father is asleep

The mother always says Dad
                  needs his sleep (his feet)

In the end hover over
                the parental bed, you angel

Pass the phone
            little child

And it's the death
                wind so howl, the hospital
                what do you do now

27.

Low sun on the rim

of the jar where the salesman

climbed in

28.

The people at the funeral are feeling dead.
That's why they don't want to be seen together.
They circle like a storm brewing in the carpark
of the dead white 60s stucco church.
The parishioners are in their coats and faces.
The chiefs of industry are in black and their wives'
handkerchiefs are like seagulls pecking at oysters.
Above, seagulls wheel on their pathway to the sea.
On the outer terrace are the thin men in jeans,
cocks zipped, waistcoats high on acid, smoking,
and the girls' breasts are cheese in muslin.
A truckload of hippies rocks up like hark hark.
They are hay thrown and look out through their hair.

In the church the family dots about the front pews
as if Jesus opened with the Queen's Gambit.
Under his baleful mosaic stare, the pine shrieks –
stations fly up the walls like shot ducks.
The priest lilts up and down, his pub poetry.
Sometimes everything goes as quiet as underwater,
but then the choir busts out. The choir is a sonar
detecting sadness, and people cry.
In the foyer I see my classmates unexpectedly
like running into them in a lesbian bar,
fancy meeting you here.

At the wake you can tell that everyone has died,
because no one cares about death anymore.
They drink and talk and laugh into the night.
Where you left the body in the earth that afternoon
the sexton will have been and made a mound
arching towards heaven.

29.

One two
three four

party on a Monday
injured on Tuesday

we don't want your
died on Wednesday

racist war
buried on Friday

that was the end of
Philip Kennedy.

30.

I am watching the materialists who have no materials
the loved Gen X, Y, Z,
schooled in the alphabet of desire, they finger seamlessly the black window,
anti-moths at a dark pane.
They are silent – or their moth screams are inaudible to the human ear,
their headphones high quality.
They live on the side of the screen that has no materials, yet they are
materialists,
so the situation is very sad.
There is probably nothing on the other side either, but who cares? We are here,
and they have no materials.
If they were nonmaterialists and had no materials that might work.
But unfortunately, they are materialists.
Forgive me if this sounds ironic. I'm not trying to be funny, although I realise
that's almost impossible these days.
I want to be the Winston Smith of seriousness, to recall the last shreds of
seriousness
before they also become funny.
Sometimes, if you walk along Great North Road at sunset blinded by the glare
through your hair, and by traffic
and keep looking into the blinding world, an old serious thought comes up.
The materialists have no materials
except for their bodies which they couldn't get by without. Their bodies are
mashable
and tender and those very qualities
are both sad and heartwarming. The tenderness of the body is actually the
whole point.
The materialists have no materials.
Oh, they do have a bedroom. Their room is dark, still and moist like a
mushroom farm
or farm for thoughts
which are like moths. Like, there are no moths, then suddenly they are
everywhere.

(Some materialists of course
have no bedroom and must live under a bridge or in a doorway or in a car
and those people
already know the perils of materialism with no materials, those people arguably
are not even materialists
anymore. Those people do not need to bother reading this poem.)
I am watching the materialists.
They follow avidly shadows moving on the screen, and they kill this guy and this guy
using their opposable thumbs.
The thumbs are how all this started. And they kill another guy and another,
they shoot them dead and they shoot
more and more until at the end of the afternoon, although it's hard to tell day from night,
bodies like slugs litter the screen
which might sound like gratuitous violence, but in fact it is all in a good cause:
a story, and a good one.
For materialists with no materials, a good story is everything because it is portable,
lightweight, and relatively inexpensive,
like the air we breathe. Although sometimes the materialists watch a documentary
on the screen in the middle of the night
about how in the future air may not be so cheap and so accessible,
it might be hard to come by
especially if the methane in the oceans heats to a certain point and explodes.
Then air will be like tulips
in Holland in the eighteenth century or like Ikea in New Zealand, or worse,
and they worry like hell about that.
They watch disaster movies so disastrous they have to watch them
with their bodies twisted into a ball
(and remember their bodies are tender), so this is not good, it is stressful
watching a world being destroyed
on the other side of the screen in the middle of the night, and the materialists
get very worried
because worlds are material, and materials are the materialists' stock-in-trade
even though they don't have any,
or many. But the movies must be watched because an unwatched movie
is even scarier. How would
the materialists know all the catastrophes that could befall the earth otherwise?

How could they be prepared
for an ice age or the sea exploding? Actually, there isn't much they can do
apart from lobby government
to reduce emissions, and especially lobby the most powerful government in the world,
but that is for the daytime,
and they don't even live in the powerful country, they live in a small country
and it is the middle of the night,
which it often is, and the movie is only a story. Stories are their stock-in-trade,
the materialists without any materials.
Without stories they would die; I tell you they would die. I tell you solemnly,
without stories they would die.
You might think the materialists with no materials sit around all day and night
playing games and watching movies
with their tender bodies twisted into a ball, but no, they go to school.
Well, air-school. They study
Philosophy, which is interesting but it makes them worry even more.
They worry that in the future
there will be nothing to apply Philosophy to, on either side of the screen.
They worry there will be no food,
no water, no air. No materials whatsoever, and for materialists that is frightening.
So they do vocational training,
something too complicated to explain but you have to follow it like a game
except it is not fun.
They are like border terriers bred to catch rats except they will probably
live in the city where there are
not many rats, and someone will have to take them for walks for exercise
so they don't get depressed
and they worry about who will take them for walks. Who will take them?
They learned the violin
but have no strings. They learned biology but they have no healthcare, botany
but they cannot grow food.
They learned nutrition, but one corporation owns almost all the supermarkets.
They hate that, they hate it,
but there's nothing you can do but lobby government especially the most powerful
government in the world,
but they don't live in the powerful country, and it is the middle of the night.

I am watching the materialists
who have no materials. The materials they had they spent on the piece of paper
that says they can metaphorically
hunt rats, but there are no rats. The materialists float in Purgatorio with the ghosts
of indentured labourers
the plantation workers who could never save enough to go home, the students
who can never pay off their debt
and go home. They watch the screen. The screen is sometimes beautiful,
a lake in a dark forest,
obsidian shining in the flank of a rock. They will love this, you will love this.
But they cannot have it.
They will find true love, but they cannot meet anyone, outlandish sex
but they find they don't find
the person attractive in person. They can vote, but fuck everything,
everything is fucked.
The screen is a fringe of hair through which the materialists view the sunset.
You might think the materialists
with no materials are thoughtless – you might think that precisely because
they have no materials,
they have no expensive bullshit machine. Remember they are the materialists
who are not racist, they are
the materialists who are okay with LGBTQIAPK, they are the materialists
who are okay with everybody
except they don't get the chance to show it because they are materialists
with no materials.
You might think they are self-centred, and you might think that precisely
because they have no power,
they have no real estate apart from their egos, they have no platform
apart from their bedroom
(if they have a bedroom), there is nothing out there for them because they are
materialists without materials.
And this is where it gets particularly sad and unfair: for their whole lives
they have been peddled materials
while at the same time the means to buy materials has been taken away,
and taken away exponentially,
taken away in an escalating manner which matches the escalation of wealth

for a few, so the pattern
of taking away is an anti-pattern, a pattern that disappears into the earth.
And the extremely sad and unfair thing
is that the taking away is being executed by the generation who invented
the counterculture, the former swingers
who believed in community, authenticity and peace, who believed in
youth culture for fuck's sake,
but who came swinging back on a pendulum like a wrecking ball
and knocked the next generation
out of the very arena where they perform their egregious and foul
acts of capitalism,
and they continue as if they are the last generation on earth. The generations
keep coming,
moving through the alphabet like hurricanes: X, Y, Z. But instead of protecting
the next generation,
the people who once believed in community, authenticity, peace and youth,
they lock them in their rooms
with the things they have sold them, their screens and the hopes and dreams
that come pouring forth
from the screens like false gods. The materialists with no materials
have been fed the rice of desire,
they worship at the feet of illusion. They are eaters of beauty
but there is no beauty.
The materialists with no materials will be kept safe by their materials,
and of course there is no safety,
they look through their black screens at a brilliant future,
but there is no future.
The materialists with no materials have been trained like bears to dance
in their unbearable bedrooms,
they have been educated in the decisions of want, the deeds of desire.
I am watching
the materialists who have no materials. I am watching intently
like a capitalist, and I hope
that they will hurl themselves again and again at the screen,
burst through the screen
and collect their imaginary mind.

31.

They have taken all the flowers and they are running in the opposite direction of
    flowers going, Hell yes!
They have taken the faded photographs of friendship and they are running in the opposite
    direction of friendship going, Hell yes!
They have taken the feeling of grass and divided it among the bars of gates and they are
    going, Hell yes!
They have taken *put me in a jar* and they are running off with the jar.
They have taken *Put Me in the Zoo* and they are running off with the zoo.
They are the greatest egos of my generation and they are going,
    Hell yes!
They are cracking the delicate egos of young people like eggshells.
They are luring children into rooms and sliding the doors shut and driving away.
They are treating hens like walled-up contemplatives and they are selling their prayers.
They are using the falsetto breaks of stockbrokers to frack every song.
They have taken the potatoes and removed the eyes and sold the eyes back to
    blind farmers.
They have got the farmers to join a gang or they will sleep with the fishes.
They have taken *corporation* which once referred to the stomach of a rich man who ate a lot
    of meat like Henry VIII and run off with it and made it into the stomach of a CEO
    and they are going, Hell yes!
And supermarkets and hospitals the makers of clothes and everything you need for your body
    is run from the stomach of a rich man.
Universities are running off with the money and intellects of young people and are run
    by the stomach of a rich man.
They are telling you to put everything you think into your purse and in your purse is
    all that is lost.
They have taken new ideas and they have run with it as a marvellous idea.
They have taken *The Book of Tea* and made it about tea.

They have taken the air that comes through the airholes and raised its temperature.
    No air no air no air no air.

They have taken peace and locked it behind a gate.

They have made the windowsill wide and luxurious, but it is only for the dew.
    They have made luxuries of a floor, a roof, walls.
    They have oiled the ledge of decency.

They prop up cathedrals with the flying buttresses of tax loops.

They will force people to write poems about them and that will break poetry.

They will break everything good ending in y.
    Why why why!
    Wai wai wairua.

If I keep going with this poem, I will break poetry.

I am driven to break this book, this paper and the forestry industry and every word ending in y. I will break philosophy and psychotherapy.

I am a Boomer.
    Philip is my Virgil. Do not follow them into hell!
    This is my description of hell.
    You are a Boomer and you say yes to everything.
    Hell yes is a description of the terraces of purgatory and the rings of hell.

I have smudged the sunset with ash.
    I have painted the bottle shop blue.

You.

You have taken your imaginary mind but you must take it back.

Safe in its prison that thing you took.

With your opposable thumbs oppose capitalism.

32.

The present pulls the plug on the present moment by moment

Hands fly to the black tiles like pigeons to a rooftop

The objects in the room join a passing train

The thoughts in the room climb aboard a train

The temperature is high and low and indifferent

Temuera and Eileen! I'm with you on the internet

The hottest January drips like a water sculpture

Brass is green and grass is brown

The coldest July is through a shattered windscreen

Meteorologists and the homeless give a fuck

A woman feeds cats on the galeforce corner

I'm with you on the internet

A satellite like a god indicates your whereabouts

Sadness rises like silt after an earthquake

How fucked it was before civil rights

Happiness struggles out from your outrage

Pretty weeds bust over the plastic roof

You want greenness but hate gardening

I'm with you on the internet

A bedroom is like a jar for an insect

Through the curtain light grows and dies

Light runs up a beach and recedes

The things in your room are on or off like settings

I wish your lot were running everything

I am with you in spirit

I'm with you on the internet

The house is dissolved like a sixteenth-century monastery

Where you laid down your head is thin air

Where the dog ran in a figure eight is air

On the street is wilderness and newness

The movers know us better than we know ourselves

The theme has ceased to reign over its unruly offspring

Look through your sunset hair at the remains

I'm with you on the internet

The air is bright from the invisible ocean

The sea is behind a wall of corporations

What you can't see you must imagine

What you can see you cannot imagine

People look into the next moment like a pool

You are a citizen of the Pacific but it's complicated

During childbirth I sang *om* to relieve pain

A song is a pathway to the sea

A song is an internet between people

I'm with you on the internet

Nothing can shock you anymore nothing

There's a numbness in the hands and feet

An enormous message to very few people

Meaningless words for the whole of humanity

This is probably the crescendo of the world

The thing you don't want to do is wonderful

The thing you don't want to do is so bright

The thing you don't want to do is what you have been waiting for

I'm with you on the internet

I will meet you at the house in the days of recollection

I will meet you where you laid your head as a baby

I will meet you where we have imagined we will meet

33.

When you go outside after a lifetime indoors
                you skip like a lamb imagining a field

The world is glittering and you tumble into it
                and you remember this fall from before

The films you saw
                will plait together with conversations in cafes in the 80s

Plain things are beautiful, such as a scrubbed table
                and beauty is an object you cradle in your arms

A minute is a jar for your fragments

A walk with a dog soars like lampposts
                and the sky is orange

The streets, the trees, the houses are imaginary
                and your imagination is your wakefulness

The leaves, paper, a pen are an armful
                You can't fathom why they are things

Would you not think if they did not exist?

On the lake is a thought you once had
                It's a boat going out

Each day is a hole in your imagination
                Like a star in the dark sky

You can be triumphant
                but only in music and your imagination.

The light pours onto the windowsill

At sunset I tell you solemnly
                         we must look,

we must imagine
                 It is the end.

THE *THÉ*

The revolution is in the simple room.

        The window looks out on silence.

                The young men and women drink the earth.

    The lens of the tea is shimmering.

           Their young bodies are watery.

Beauty is the thing that's going *surprise*!

      The silk vest is returning to the moth.

           A thought is a Trojan horse in the head.

An hour re-forms as a cloud.

           His whole life in the folds of hills.

The little city is anchored by journeys.

       The bottom of the world is dished like a crucible.

              The people collect the drip of news.

A choir practises for the one moment.

           I am very scared of what happened yesterday.

The plates of the earth will never be content.

      A Mason jar magnifies the room.

              The salt lake goes back in time.

A ritual relieves the people of decision.

                                              Tea flowed west with the equinox!

An hour is spent with his hands in his sleeves.

The five brothers ran on the grass.

                      Moths struggle in the dusk like flowers.

                                   The soughing of pines is heard in our kettle.

The six handles congratulate the coffin.

                            There is no god only a procession.

                                    Philosophy smiles down on the thinkers.

The feet are faithful to the earth.

                            The carillon occupies an hour of light.

The pub cheers when the war is over.

                        The wind sweeps the leaves from a path.

    The despicable priest lies straight in a grave.

                                       The revolution is hatched at school.

The exquisite corpse drinks in the Duke.

                    The grey thunder booms like pride.

                    The young body is in the old ground.

Making tea is a story arc.

                              Death trickles through the cupped hands.

The young men are angry at darkness.

                    Shame causes a tide of dominoes.

                                        The rage of the poet rises like birds.

The long hour fills a bucket.

The young men wear velvet jackets.

                              The old trees are bedded in moss.

          They love the elaborate path of drugs.

                                        To him the bitter vinegar tastes sweet.

The sky is cracked like a blue vase.

                    The floating heart will never rest.

                                        I thought the library was a dream.

The parts of love are arbitrary like speech.

                    The tea room is the abode of vacancy.

A branch reaches to the right.

                                        A live flower or a painted flower?

                    The heart answers the twenty questions.

The living room is strewn with leaves.

                              The poem he wrote is bristly like a broom.

The houses on the hill are dying like trees.

                    The young flatmates fill the flimsy house.

                                        They fuck their friends in a state of flux.

The Book of Changes sets his path.

                          The cat quickly turns the page.

          The best laid plans are wait and see.

                                        They kneel to roll joints as if Japanese.

The abandoned path is loud with weeds.

                          The felted rug is out of focus.

                                        The is between yesterday and tomorrow.

The house is decorated with the dead.

                          The flies hold up a map of stars.

                                        I hesitated at the blue door.

The babies are the new grown-ups.

There is art in cleaning and dusting.

Now is the hour is hummed for an hour.

                                        Their serious thoughts ignore the harbour.

A boat worries like a dog.

                                            The new adults make contemporary art.

The disappearing tea turns up in the body.

                      An accident is a stone on the beach.

                                        To make the silk the moth must die.

On Sundays the flatmates go home for tea.

                            A street leads to the other side.

It is ready you may go through.

                                      Seagulls clock the day like bells.

They are drunk reading *The Book of Tea*.

                                  They are screwed up reading *The Book of Tea*.

They have no ritual and no GPS.

                      Lost in Wellington is like set in concrete.

                                        Rage at trivia is *too much tea*.

The Book of Tea is cool like drugs.

                      A swim would destroy their molecular structure.

                                        They wear the jackets of the dead.

The cup of humanity is their sex.

                          They fall upwards and think out loud.

The clean room is a big surprise!

                  Their bloody placards are in the passage.

                               Like beetles they digest *The Book of Tea*.

No-beginning comes back to haunt me.

                    They lug their laundry home like seamen.

They are very stoned at the parents' house.

                             They are helpless in their cool boots.

Existence is when two souls keep searching.

                            A cup of tea is kaputī.

                      Every hopeful step is hopeless.

An hour leaves the stomach behind.

When he wakes he leans on his elbow and thinks.

                               The tea slowly cools like fall.

The frost is crisp on the botanical gardens.

          A ritual basically screws deciding.

                    They step over the university.

They eat Chinese five times a week.

                The wind leaves a leaf like a Zen master.

The small passing litter is art.

        I only just left the ephemeral room.

                    The wildness in the air is red.

The house a temporary refuge of the body.

      The poem is a parking space for thoughts.

It is ready for you to go through.

      He decides to go to his proofreading job.

                    A paper house is destroyed in a storm.

They are angry at the concept *no-beginning*.

                The smashed glass makes fugitive blood.

Through the big window the Southern Cross.

        Turning the page of a book is a meme.

                    Being straight is *not enough tea*.

I woke and saw a spider on the wall.

                        The power has gone and the flat is sepia.

Deceit steals hours from a day.

           Anxiety is faithful to the earth.

                        The flatmates' coats go down the zigzag.

They send their thoughts into their pockets.

                    At Parliament their fugitive chant.

           Pō atarau e moea iho nei.

The Book of Tea in the dirty house.

                The winter afternoon is drunk.

                          They wear the traditional smile of the thief.

The unlit room has no makeup.

                        Meditation is practice at eternity.

Going for a walk is a retro thing.

           The cup is full of oblivion.

                        The world of the liquid enters the body.

Their coats have pockets under the breath.

                              The *I Ching* transforms the onionskin.

Each smoke is a bit different and leads to newness.

                    Funny and terrible like Yin and Yang.

                              The imagination may go through.

An hour in the gardens falls from the world.

                         The books they steal are written for them.

The loss leads to the next moment.

                    The dark appears to cool the lake.

                                        The poem adjusts the room.

The poem burns off an hour.

                         We walk along the street many times.

The street is practice for death.

                         The chairs are aching in and out.

                                        He staggers to his feet.

          The the is ready to go through.

Ritual finally occupies the body.

                    Thoughts burst the shelter of the room.

                              The people swarm into the streets.

The patterned life is now chaos.

                                          The blue twilight could be dawn.

                The last hour the imagined hour.

PATTERN/CHAOS: AN AFTERWORD

Death is the sanction of everything the storyteller can tell. He has borrowed his authority from death.
— Walter Benjamin, 'The Storyteller'

One afternoon in the late sixties, our mother Veronica impulse-bought a beautiful and expensive red Persian rug. Splashing out was almost unheard of for her — not that she needed to be cautious about money; it was boom times, and we were comfortably middle class — but she had grown up poor through the Depression and the habits of frugality die hard. On this day, however, as she walked through Wellington city, she was stopped by an intricate pattern in a shop window, one that seemed to draw her in (so she described later), and for some reason she threw thrift to the wind. Within hours, the heavy roll was being delivered to our house on the shoulder of a puffing man and unfurled on top of the carpet in the sitting room. The rug was dark and lush, and the ends still curled slightly like the headdress of a Pasifika chief. Veronica patted it as if it were a cat and walked on it experimentally in her stockinged feet, unaccustomedly wide-eyed. 'It's from Iran,' she said, as if to chalk the whole enterprise up to exoticism. Like a magic carpet, the rug from Iran did seem to transport her briefly to some other realm — which was good because she'd seemed harried lately, and you need your mum to be happy. The cause of her sad face was no secret to anyone, least of all herself: 'the teenagers'. There were several of them, and they were a pain in the arse. Within five years one of them would be dead. Veronica's wild purchase that day was, probably, her single act of retail therapy.

With a ring of stern rattan armchairs looking on, the rug filled the walk-space in the sitting room and somehow tolerated the threadbare beige floral carpet showing on its perimeter. The Persian pattern was a rich ruby geometry, the pile fine and perfectly shorn like a number-four haircut, the fringe at either end an ecru silk. I ventured out onto the soft red in my white school socks, an act that felt strangely radical, especially as our little world was already in flux — it was post-Vatican II, we had decimal currency, and the Beatles had broken up. Now, with the dusty unknowable tone of my parents' pre-war aesthetic receding fast, even Veronica had made a statement. Nothing made sense; it was diabolical but exciting.

I was to get to know the nature of the new rug very well, because for hours on end I had it to myself. Although the house was chaotic with people – like a factory, there was a night shift; teenagers bashed pans around in the kitchen and fell over drunk in the passage – the sitting room was your traditional, infrequently used parlour, and for some reason the two youngest members of the family were free to occupy it. We occupied it separately. Richard – three years older than me and even as a tween a true musician – practised guitar in there several hours a day. The rest of the time, the space was mine. Over ten years, I used the rug as desk, chair and couch.

From the doorway, the pattern seemed relatively simple: a series of red rectangles laid end to end that formed a wide path around a central no-person's land containing an oval universe-shaped burst. As if to be practical, I wasn't interested in the Big Bang, only in the surrounding pattern and its teeming rectangles. Each one was filled with uniform flourishes in navy blue and dark green, all with shots of tiger-eye yellow. But up close, when you sat or lay down on the rug, it became apparent that things were more complex than first thought; you couldn't tell whether the curls and blurry details of each rectangle were the same or just similar. I would sometimes crawl over the wool – which wasn't prickly but silky smooth to touch – comparing the iterations of pattern and hoping to solve some kind of riddle. But by the time I'd studied several of them, I couldn't remember exactly how the first one had been, or even which rectangle I'd started at. That was the fascination; it was involving and endless. When you stood up, the red Persian rug sprang back into sameness and symmetry, but because you'd looked closely, the pattern would never trick you into the idea of simplicity again.

I have this rug now under my dining table. Being last in the pattern of children and one who didn't emigrate, I'm the receptacle for many things from the family house. Over time, the rug has changed. For one thing, its status as an artefact from Iran – two Gulf Wars on and in a time of US isolationism – is less Orientalist and more overtly troubling. Of course, after fifty years, the rug is worn and it has faded to a particular strawberry red. A few years ago I cut off the almost nonexistent fringe, intending to get it rebound at least, but I never did. As a puppy, the dog once chewed a corner. The rectangles were long ago trodden threadbare. Now there is no point even trying to work out any variations in pattern; sameness and difference have been written over by feet, light and decay.

The red Persian rug reminds me of the musical form of variations for two reasons: one, because the pattern on the rug *is* variations; and two, there was the particular six-month period in my early teens during which I listened to Beethoven's *Thirty-Three Variations on a Waltz by Anton Diabelli*, op. 120 over and over while stretched out on the wool. Sometimes when things line up – events, objects – it can seem as if we're part of a giant pattern. I find it comforting to think that from time to time, otherwise it's just chaos.

Listening to the *Diabelli Variations* then – knowing nothing apart from what my ears told me – I soon worked out there was some kind of experiment in patterning going on, which *sounds* like a contradiction in terms, and partly is. The structure of musical variations is, broadly speaking, 'change within limits', but what those alterations might bring, who can predict? A small original template – a tune, a theme – is replicated again and again but with changes each time of key, metre, tempo and style. The original theme evolves bit by bit, but in steps incremental enough for the listener to be able to follow its path, remember its origin and regard the whole series as one cycle. Later I learned that some variations were written as studies or practice pieces, but most were intended to be listened to as a formal work, just as I listened formally on the rug. I got to know the variations' 'top of the pops', including Bach's *Goldberg Variations*, Brahms' *Variations on a Theme of Haydn* and Rachmaninov's *Variations on a Theme of Corelli* (all men, although each man different from the last). I was struck by the fact I couldn't predict how the pattern would evolve.

In 1961, scientist Edward Lorenz suggested that when a small difference (like a butterfly beating its wing) is applied to initial conditions, the effect can be enormous over time. We should be able to predict the outcome, but because of the scale we cannot. Chaos, according to Lorenz, occurs when 'the present determines the future, but the approximate present does not approximately determine the future'.

If we begin with a shred of tune, a ditty, and replicate it in a chain of subtly different musical ways, we should be able to predict the outcome, but we can't. That instability is what is inherently experimental about the form of variations, even in its strictly patterned Baroque clothes like the Bach. Variations – they might also be called transformations – resound inevitably into something we could never have imagined: they flower, they surge forth into the new. Without those incremental steps there would be no 'work', just a fragment. How poor we would be without change.

I can't remember who the pianist was on the recording of the *Diabelli Variations* that I thrashed back in 1973–74. Later I listened to the stupendous version by the great Alfred Brendel, who wrote:

> The theme has ceased to reign over its unruly offspring. Rather, the variations decide what the theme may have to offer them. Instead of being confirmed, adorned and glorified, it is improved, parodied, ridiculed, disclaimed, transfigured, mourned, stamped out and finally uplifted.

I could never have guessed the way things would unravel, set in motion by the terrible event that occurred in our family in 1973.

Beethoven's *Diabelli Variations* is widely considered the most exalted manifestation of the variation form. When I was fourteen I didn't know that, nor did I understand why I felt so stirred in the midst of its forty minutes. Now I know a few things; I know things pass. I know that this composition goes bananas: it reaches out in invention, importing musical ideas from outside the gambit of the theme; it ends up far away from where it began. Written between 1819–23 for solo piano, and based on a simple and frankly silly waltz by Diabelli – papa *pum*pumpum *pum*pumpum *pum*pumpum *pum*pum – the *Diabelli Variations* (thirty-three, for the number of years Jesus lived) is Beethoven's last major piano work, and it seems to have 'bucket list' written all over it. Firstly, the piano is scragged to within an inch of its life with furious poundings, tortured chromaticism and hocketty rhythms. If Beethoven had ever encountered a prepared piano (à la John Cage), I think he would have approved, because in the *Diabelli Variations*, he is trying to make the piano do something it almost couldn't manage.

He is also declaring himself fairly and squarely a Romantic. Beethoven started life as a Classicist like Mozart and ended as a Romantic like, say, Brahms. His oeuvre bridges the enormous gap between the expected and the unexpected, from pattern to freedom. As a Classicist, he employed the 'hero's journey' approach to key and theme – to wander from home in an increasingly tense-making, elastic way, to encounter obstacles, deal with them, and then, with some new insight, return home. The built-in narrative arc imposes a comforting sense of structure to the unavoidable tour. If only life were like sonata form!

But in the *Diabelli Variations*, Beethoven breaks free of such constraints, and as the Romantic, takes the notion of 'tour' to a new level. For one thing, where the Classical model was usually to journey through a series of related keys, he keeps mostly to C major (the simplest, happiest key) and experiments with everything else – with chromaticism, with form and style. He seems to be saying: what you think you know, you do not know.

But the most extraordinary departure Beethoven makes in the *Diabelli Variations* is to suggest that our journey is the one we have already taken; we aren't so much the hero, in control and making decisions about how to act: we are the product of our surroundings. And so instead of exploring key or even theme, the *Diabelli Variations* wander among the vastness of Beethoven's musical influences. The individualistic lonely journey seems like an early warning for modernism.

This all might sound very serious; however, the *Diabelli Variations* began as something of a spoof. The story goes that Diabelli had asked a group of composers to write variations on his theme (the then equivalent of bragging on social media), and while initially Beethoven declined he later changed his mind. From the first few jokily pompous variations it seems clear that Beethoven despised the bouncy tune with the same ten notes in a row, and then another ten (it grew on me, by the way, like a pop song), and he took the piss. But what starts out as hilarity gets more and more profound; Beethoven has something to say about life, about music and about politics. A supporter of Napoleon (the *Eroica* symphony celebrates his rise), Beethoven believed in a modern Europe. The *Diabelli Variations* is a gathering of forces, of musical countries.

What Beethoven did for variations as a form was to expose its wild nature – that the iterations may travel somewhere unimagined, like Lorenz's small, gallant, chaotic changes. Of course, these changes were possible all along; Beethoven lets his musical knowledge, his artefacts, lead him on. This is the music of his life, and therefore of mortality. Like Mozart's *Requiem*, the *Diabelli Variations* is a work facing eternity.

At fourteen, I couldn't think this, but I felt it.

Now, more than forty years later, inspired by the *Diabelli Variations* (my 1974 soundtrack), I remember my brother's death. I have delved among Philip's story, his books and writings, and my own museum, to see where it takes me. I have written Philip's history, or it wrote me.

The poem, 'Come catch me little child', was part of the collection Philip wrote in his late teens. At the time of his death in 1973, so the story goes, the manuscript had been accepted by publisher Alister Taylor, who had launched Sam Hunt and had recently brought out *The Little Red Schoolbook* and Tim Shadbolt's *Bullshit and Jellybeans*. I don't know if this is true. (Ten years later, Taylor would go bankrupt.) In any case, Philip's little volume was never a published book, but the manuscript survives. Like the red rug from Iran, I have it in my possession.

It has not been my intention to tell Philip's life story but to respond to his poem because Philip was a serious poet. To do that, however, I need to do forensics on what the poem came out of – Philip's poetics, his politics and some notion of how it was to be a young adult in the late sixties and early seventies. 'Come catch me' didn't come out of thin air; the times constituted their own strong brew. Forty-five years on, what also interests me is what became of the ideals of the world Philip lived in; they were high ideals, but they have been subsumed and overwritten by the very generation who produced them, like a snake that feasts on its own tail.

First, Exhibit A: The poetry manuscript Philip left behind is tracked with the footsteps of other poets and writers. It's a kind of 'exquisite corpse' (like the Surrealists' game of word collage) constructed from the contents of his bookcase and more. In a moment I'll revisit those shelves, but for the meantime, the bookends will suffice: at one end, late James K. Baxter (of course), cool as a cucumber in his vernacular clothes; at the other end (perhaps more surprisingly), Gertrude Stein, all languagey and mad; one of the poems in Philip's collection is simply, 'Mayhap I will not talk about it otherwise'. Of the others, some are plain-speaking polemics (Baxterish), but many are semi-lush (and maybe drunken) romantic channellings of not one but two Dylans – Dylan Thomas and Bob Dylan. The collection as a whole has the energetic spring of a young person wishin' and hopin' and thinkin', and is inspired not just from the page, but from music. (Definitely not prayin', though; Philip had had more than enough of that.) The last line of 'Come catch me' and the theme for this book – 'and collect your imaginary mind' – suggests that we will find some solution if only we keep searching in the places we can't see. In these terrible times that thought alone makes me hopeful; it restores my belief in the constructive purpose of writing and imagining. And I want to know more about where that sentiment came from, and how and why it died an untimely death.

Philip was something of a hippie, not that he would have called himself that – hippie was the term other people used. But he did have long hair, wore brightly coloured pants and a waistcoat. He had a poster of Che Guevara on his wall as a teenager, and had a penchant for altering his mind artificially. He was a man of his times. In 1964 there had been no hippies; by 1967 there were hundreds of thousands in San Francisco, and by 1969 ('The Summer of Love'), the movement was all through the Western world, including Wellington. From what I remember of conversations round the dinner table, and from the group of hairy young men slouched in armchairs who seemed to live at our house (including Philip's close friend, the poet Geoff Cochrane), they were heavily engaged with everything the new progressiveness held dear – opposition to fifties austerity, civil rights, the relaxation of censorship (of the 'Hays Code') and the rise of sexual freedom. If little New Zealand, a gnat-like American ally, was to be roped into the conditions of a post-isolationist US – capitalism, the invasion of Vietnam, the overriding Cold War and the Bomb – then we would also be party to any response. That's how imperialism works.

To Philip and his cohort – white, hovering around the middle class, educated like their American hippie counterparts, angry about all of the above, hanging out in Wellington with nothing much to do but read their parents' copies of *The Saturday Evening Post* (specially flown in) – the tenets of the counterculture must have soothed like Tiger Balm. What was not to like about authenticity, individualism, community? And, to sugar the pill if those essentialist concepts sounded slightly like hard work: music, a fascination with Eastern spirituality and drugs.

This, anyway, is what I imagine.

On leaving school in 1968, Philip did what any self-respecting hippie would do: he dropped out of higher education. (I hold the highly educated Timothy Leary personally responsible for all but one of my brothers not going to university.) From then on, Philip's learning went its own way, which is not to say it stopped because hippies worked from a theoretical basis. But as with their clothes, candles and dope, it was homegrown. So there's another quality I think I can detect in 'Come catch me little child' – wildness. (Which also might come from living at Island Bay, a mile from the bright windy coast at the bottom of the North Island.)

In any case, hippiedom was not to last, even if its reach is still strong in New Zealand Pākehā culture. Although looking back it seems obvious, by 1971 the movement was hitting a strange T-junction with postmodernism and capitalism. Poor Philip and his friends had to navigate a shaky border between the modern and post-, which is perhaps similar to the Classical and Romantic doorstep Beethoven traversed – each a vast cultural shift. Could life get any more complicated than Mozart meets Wagner? Than the Buddha meets Monty Python? Well, yes. According to W. J. Rorabaugh, the hippie tenet of individualism (which never *did* fit with community) was following its natural path back towards libertarianism. And that is exactly what has happened.

But Philip remains in 1973. He is a snapshot from history. We want the poet to be influencing the future, don't we, and not the other way around? But I would not have access to these poems if Philip had lived. I would not be sitting here assuming that once doubt was cast on the moving parts of the counterculture – authenticity, individualism, community – what Philip and his cohort were left with was outrage and the imagination. To me, both seem good conditions for a poet. If his belief in poetry was anything to go by, it seemed he had embraced, in the words of Japanese art critic Kakuzo Okakura, 'the subtle use of the useless'.

I do, too. I want to look back at 'Come catch me', not just because of the tragedy of my brother's death (to remember him), but because the poem itself exhorts us to open up to the imagination and reminds us of something we need more than ever: hopefulness.

Philip was born on 10 May 1951, the fifth child of eight (one child died as a baby), and brought up in what was essentially a Catholic enclave in Wellington – mostly Irish but also Italian and Polish. He was bright at school, interested in history, went wild in his teens, then started to come right. At the time of his death he was due to take up a position as a junior reporter at a provincial newspaper, but he never made it.

Philip suffered from grand mal epilepsy, a serious brain dysfunction which was controlled as well as it could be at the time by the drug Phenobarbital. A few times a year he would forget to take his pills for a day or, as was the rumour, decide not to take them as a statement about something-or-other. Watching the result of Philip off his meds was to understand the part 'seize' plays in 'seizure'. Philip's body would be gripped by a seemingly demonic force. He would be hurled to the floor in a jerking paroxysm, his limbs pulsating as if alive with electricity; an epileptic seizure is a kind of brain short-circuit. His mouth would clench and there was the fear he would swallow his tongue – since proved to be a myth. But in those days it was considered a likely way for him to die, so people would rush to put things in his mouth: pencils, spoons, and one time, reputedly, a friend's finger which was thoroughly mangled. (How wrong we are about so many things; maybe everything is wrong.) After the epileptic episode, Philip would be walked in a zombie-like state to his bed, where he would sleep deeply all day (the attacks seemed to mostly occur in the morning). He would wake at dusk, blinking and subdued as if coming out of an anaesthetic, or waking up to a new world, with no idea what had happened or that any time had passed. He would be quiet for several hours, which was eerie; quietness was not his usual state. If he could have witnessed one of his fits – if someone could have filmed it on a phone – he would never have missed a single dose of medication.

Seen from a doorway (like the view of my mother's rug), Philip's epilepsy looked like a kind of rage. It's worth considering that trauma lay behind Philip's quest for answers, a quest he pursued through poetry. While sexual abuse stories from Catholic schools continue to come forward, the plight of children who suffered extreme physical violence at these schools has not yet been documented. But I think it can be acknowledged, based on phenomenological evidence, that thousands of children, mostly boys, were subject to trauma-inducing physical abuse from priests in those schools, and Philip was no exception. Indeed, because he was outspoken (perhaps a gifted child with particular needs), his education at the hands of Marist priests was appallingly abusive. Most of my brothers lived for years with loathing and terror of their schools. I remember the carnival atmosphere in our house the day the news came through that a particularly sadistic priest from the primary school had died.

Phenobarbital might have mostly controlled Philip's seizures, but it had side effects, as we now know. Two effects are irritability and anxiety, which might explain Philip's occasional wild moods. Another is dizziness, so the drug may have contributed to the fall down a bank at the party, the fall that killed him. After his death, when people were remembering the small characteristics of Philip that would never be seen again, it was recalled that whenever he got up from a chair, he staggered backwards for a few seconds until he could gain his equilibrium. That little stagger before being properly upright seemed to be the endearing essence of Philip. Until one day, the stagger was not enough.

When he was eighteen he went to Queen Mary Hospital at Hanmer Springs near Christchurch to dry out. At least, that was the term our mother used. With a strange mixture of shame, relief and pride she explained his absence to a few close people, neighbours and such, and to the family: Philip had 'gone down south to dry out'. I pictured him pinkly waterlogged and swollen, sitting on a map of the mainland of New Zealand. 'Dry out' was a tidy way of describing the therapy Philip was clearly in need of. The siblings now, looking back, remember Philip as not drinking more than anyone else – sure, he drank like a fish but he lived in an aquarium. Still, there's no doubt he had run amok. He was angry. He didn't work. He was convicted for stealing records from a shop. (To give him his due, it was the fashion among his group; how else would you get records? He would've loved file sharing.)

The escapades brought enormous shame on the family – 'a Catholic boy!' – and I think it's safe to say Philip was responsible for our mother buying a ridiculous rug one desperate afternoon. It seems likely that the side effects of Phenobarbital mixed with alcohol played havoc with his brain chemistry. Whatever the reasons behind his spell there, the hospital was good for Philip. He came back from Hanmer Springs changed, older-seeming, motivated, even-tempered. Our mother would often say he'd been inspired by Sir Charles Burns who was medical officer at Queen Mary's at the time. Like some kind of angel, it was as if a good seizure had taken hold of him and he'd woken up as a new person.

After Hanmer, Philip got on with it. Abandoning Timothy Leary, he took a job as a proofreader, talked about studying, invited family members out to lunch one by one with his new-found pay packet – including me, age twelve in a Chinese restaurant. He told me he woke up early 'to think'. He may have been on step something-or-other, the one about 'Sorry', and come to think of it, it had been pretty tough being around Philip when he was on alcohol-marijuana-Phenobarbital cocktails with umbrellas in them. By that time, anyway, the ideals of the age were turning like leaves. The euphoria of hippiedom, having sprung up so quickly was already dying. For Philip, it seems, released from an ideological package, poetry was now his drug ('I think in the mornings'), and he wrote his manuscript.

After Philip's death, there was just a handful of his belongings gathered at the family house where I, aged fourteen, still lived. He had not accrued many possessions in his short life, and I imagine Philip's things would have been regarded by his friends and flatmates as a kind of village common. His iconic tooled leather bag, for instance, which had come home from the hospital after his death and hung on the Victorian coat hooks outside the bathroom, disappeared during the wake, which upset our parents. The bag lived on as if it still hung on its curly iron hook; if it had not been taken, I would not remember it now. Because there were so few things, and there would be no more, each object assumed great importance as if boosted by some mortality index: 'Philip's books', 'Philip's communion medal', 'Philip's bag'. There was a tiny ornamental angel in the china cabinet which had always been known as 'Philip's angel' (none of the other siblings had their own angel). This angel now bore his name indelibly.

Peter is the brother closest in age to Philip. He was also one of the flatmates at Patanga Crescent, Philip's last address (the Māori word 'patanga' means 'advantage' or 'benefit'). Of the siblings, he was the most devastated at the loss of Philip. It was he who brought Philip's books back to the childhood bookcase at Island Bay.

On the man-height bookcase – a kind of statue – part of the man remained. I retired to the Persian rug and read, gradually: *Pig Island Letters*, *Jerusalem Sonnets*, *Autumn Testament*, *The Ballad of Calvary Street* and *Ode to Auckland*, by James K. Baxter (Baxter had himself died the year before Philip at age forty-six); *New Poems*, by Günter Grass; *Borstal Boy*, by Brendan Behan; *The Psychedelic Experience*, by Timothy Leary; Ralph Metzner and Richard Alpert; *The Metamorphosis*, by Franz Kafka.

Eventually, I read Philip's battered, mustard-coloured edition of *The Book of Tea*, and consulted *The Book of Changes* for advice, like an agony aunt. And quasi-religious-philosophical texts like *Autobiography of a Yogi* and *Siddhartha*. I'm guessing that Philip, being brought up Catholic and junking it at puberty (a rite of passage), was primed to at least give other beliefs and customs a whirl. I imagine him lapping up the ideals of Okakura in *Tea* – 'Teaism is Taoism in disguise' – its purity and transience, and the Zen insistence on the house as a temporary refuge for the body. A tea room, therefore, was no longer a place to have a meat pie at Taihape, nor a middle-class clutter-fest, but a fugitive place of spareness, of the single use of a shape or colour, of no-symmetry, of no-pattern. I imagine the rage at being deceived; disgust at the trappings of our bourgeois house, the cabinets like those at the Victoria and Albert Museum, the floral carpet and the oil portrait in the hall of our grandfather painted by Julia Lynch.

> We find it trying to talk to a man while his full-length portrait
> stares at us from behind his back. We wonder which is real,
> he of the picture or he who talks, and feel a curious conviction
> that one of them must be a fraud.
> (Okakura)

As the post-war generation, they'd been tricked into thinking that the Western material world was important, was worth fighting for, worth their father's PTSD (but not our father, who had a disability and was exempted from service), and worth another war in which a little girl could be seen napalmed by American-backed forces on the TV news. Something must be done; a new order must be imagined.

I also read the poems in the manila envelope.

As anyone who has lost a family member too early will know, no one in the close circle ever entirely recovers. The effect of the death resounds into the rest of your life and the life of the family in changing ways. At first no pattern is obvious. Moment follows moment, and these moments must be lived. In the stunned, slo-mo, immediate aftermath of Philip's death we each dealt with the loss differently, but all lacked the means to grieve. That lack comes via a generalised, post-industrial, Western disassociation with ritual – but there is more. We are descended from the Irish; our great-grandparents were in the first generation born in Ireland after the Great Famine to people who often did not have the energy to bury their dead. The new generation emigrated knowing they would never return and were given wakes before they embarked – another kind of death, heading out across the water like Osiris. The practices around death were all at sea.

When Philip died, we didn't know what to do. I think that's why I have written these poems. Forty-five years on (although years are nothing in the scale of things), I am singing him away with thirty-three variations. I am burying him in thirty-three layers. I have written Philip a coffin text like an ancient Egyptian writing on the interior walls of a sarcophagus. The text is for us, of course, who are still innocent.

Our reactions to grief in the family were individual and random; our dad Matt began brewing (or brewed some more of) the cancer that would kill him three years later; Veronica took the first steps into the pool of depression that eventually submerged her; Margaret Mary and James were overseas; Matthew, our intellectually disabled brother, seemed baffled and sighed a lot; Peter (a talented musician) became addicted to heroin; Richard and I, at seventeen and fourteen respectively and the only siblings younger than Philip at the time of his death, were, I suspect, too young to understand the enormity of what had happened. Partly we were protected by that. We didn't realise how tragic the loss was; how it wasn't every day that a twenty-two-year-old dies. We couldn't begin to understand how agonising it was for our parents to lose a child.

Richard listened, all day it seemed, to Julian Bream's solo guitar arrangements of Baroque hits, his one foray into 'Classical' music; all his life he has been a rock and pop musician. I listened to the *Diabelli Variations* on the portable turquoise plastic turntable in the sitting room every day for six months. I would lie on the red Persian rug, listening, smoking a cigarette (there was no supervision in our house), and fingering the soft pattern. I got to know both sets of variations, wool and music, better than I knew my grief. Then one day, as a Victorian woman changes into mauve six months after a bereavement, I moved on from the *Diabelli Variations* and didn't listen to them again until I was presented with them, like a memory card, in a university course. Then I learned how they broke the mould.

Somehow, we were able to make death normal. Which it is. Death is normal; life is strange. I (at least) could pretend some of the time that Philip's death was the doorstep to an imaginary world, the world Philip tried to make with his poetry and in particular with 'Come catch me little child'. Only in looking back can I see that Philip's death became my template for loss and art. Perhaps that is what everyone comes to in the end and it just took me a long time to realise it. Rugs wear out, people die, patterns change, and once gone they can only ever be imagined.

Finally, death has given me permission to tell this story, to quote this poem, and I pay my respects to the living and the dead.

(IIML, Wellington, 2016 – University of Iowa, 2017)

NOTES

Early versions of some of the poems from 'Thirty-Three Transformations on a Theme of Philip' first appeared in *Landfall* and on Poetry Shelf.

The version of *Thirty-Three Variations on a Waltz by Anton Diabelli*, op. 120 by Ludwig van Beethoven, which I listened to while writing this book, was recorded by Alfred Brendel, on *Beethoven: Diabelli Variations*, CD ALC1194, Alto, 2012.

All quotations by Kakuzo Okakura are from *The Book of Tea* (Dover Publications, New York, 1964).

p. xi
Lines from 'Moth Hour' by Adrienne Rich are quoted with the kind permission of W. W. Norton & Company, Inc. Copyright © 2016 by the Adrienne Rich Literary Trust. Copyright © 1966 by W. W. Norton & Company, Inc., from *Collected Poems: 1950–2012* by Adrienne Rich.

p. 9
The W. B. Yeats line 'moth-hour of eve' is from his poem 'The Ballad of Father Gilligan'.

p. 13
'Come catch me little child' is from an unpublished poetry manuscript by Philip Kennedy, *c.* 1972, in the possession of Anne Kennedy.

pp. 66 & 88
The words of Alfred Brendel are from *Music, Sense and Nonsense: Collected Essays and Lectures* by Alfred Brendel (Biteback Publishing, London, 2015), and are quoted with the kind permission of Biteback Publishing.

p. 80
'Pō atarau e moea iho nei' is from the waiata 'Now is the Hour/Pō Atarau Haere ra' by Clement Scott (music) and Maewa Kaihau (Māori lyrics).

p. 85
The Walter Benjamin quotation is from his essay 'The Storyteller: Reflections on the Works of Nikolai Leskov' from *Illuminations: Essays and Reflections* (Schocken Books, New York, 1968).

p. 87
Edward Lorenz's theory of chaos is originally from his article, 'Deterministic Nonperiodic Flow', *Journal of the Atmospheric Sciences*, vol. 20, March 1963, pp. 130–41.

p. 92
Thoughts from W. J. Rorabaugh are from *American Hippies* (Cambridge University Press, Cambridge, 2015).

ACKNOWLEDGEMENTS

My heartfelt thanks are due to: everyone at AUP, especially Sam Elworthy, Katharina Bauer and Sophia Broom; designer Kalee Jackson; everyone at the International Institute of Modern Letters (IIML), Victoria University of Wellington, where I was Writer in Residence in 2016 and had the time and space to begin *Moth Hour*; the Fall Residency of the International Writing Program at the University of Iowa, where I completed the book; Creative New Zealand for funding my stay in Iowa; the incomparable Bill Lake for songs; dear friends Anna Hodge, Chris Bourke, Katrina Duncan and Margaret Samuels for advice and encouragement; colleague and friend Caryline Boreham for photographing the moment of a moth; Temuera and Eileen, always. Arohanui.